LADY BIRD

LADY BIRD

KERRY GILBERT

EXILE
editions

singular fiction, poetry, nonfiction, translation, drama, and graphic books

Library and Archives Canada Cataloguing in Publication

Title: Lady bird / Kerry Gilbert.
Names: Gilbert, Kerry, author.
Description: Poems.
Identifiers: Canadiana (print) 2023015624X | Canadiana (ebook) 20230156274 |
    ISBN 9781990773105 (softcover) | ISBN 9781990773112 (EPUB) |
    ISBN 9781990773129 (Kindle) | ISBN 9781990773136 (PDF)
Classification: LCC PS8613.I396 L33 2023 | DDC C811/.6—dc23

Book and cover designed by Michael Callaghan
Typeset in Bembo and Granjon fonts at Moons of Jupiter Studios
Images courtesy of Purdue University Libraries, Karnes Archives and Special Collection
Printed and bound in Canada by Gauvin

Published by Exile Editions
144483 Southgate Road 14, Holstein, Ontario, N0G 2A0
www.ExileEditions.com

We gratefully acknowledge the Government of Canada and Ontario Creates
    for their financial support toward our publishing activities.

Canadä ONTARIO CREATES

Canadian sales representation: The Canadian Manda Group, 664 Annette Street,
Toronto ON M6S 2C8 www.mandagroup.com 416 516 0911

North American and international distribution, and U.S. sales:
Independent Publishers Group, 814 North Franklin Street,
Chicago IL 60610 www.ipgbook.com toll free: 1 800 888 4741

for Sharon Thesen
"everything belongs"

as a society, we bury our dead and
yet often refuse to let them die

we vacillate between fear and fascination

—Eve Joseph *In the Slender Margin*

prologue

how to survive an airplane crash

you will need an aisle seat   long-sleeved pants
closed-toe shoes   and a smoke hood or a wet washcloth

step 1: book a seat in the exit row or within five rows of it

      step 2: wear pants and a long-sleeved shirt made of
non-flammable material

          step 3: bring a smoke hood, or even just a wet
washcloth sealed in a plastic bag

            step 4: once aboard, count the seats between
you and the nearest front and rear emergency exit

               step 5:   brace yourself for landing
              feet on floor   cross arms in front

               tip: remove any sharp objects
               from your shirt and pants

               step 6: it may sound stupid
               but airplane seat belts open
               by lifting a buckle not
               pushing a button

step 7: you want
to stoop, not crawl

                              tip: exit the plane immediately
                              find your loved ones outside

        step 8: once off   run for your life—literally
get away

did you know passengers who sit near the back of the plane
are 40% more likely to survive a crash

*please know i am quite aware of the
hazards. i want to do it because i want*

*to do it. women must try to do things as
men have tried. when they fail their*

failure must be but a challenge to others
~a.e.

one

*few people realize that more than a hundred years
before the twentieth-century pioneers, there were other
women aeronauts. they did their flying in balloons*

~(a.e—the fun of it)

amelia, where did your bones go

did they have the free fall of plane and air
or the soft float sink of body and water or
the erosion of an open grave

island animals your congregation
did you have time to lament
to build a lean-to, to keep off the rain

to drink water from a folded leaf
or did your heart drop into your throat
just long enough to feel you were alive

once you flew, you really flew
did you know they wouldn't know
whether the bones were yours

the length and density of them
much, much more like a man's
and that's really it, isn't it

these things that divide us
that we shed our skin to overcome
when ultimately a bone is a bone

a skull
a humorous

radius
tibia

fibula
and both femora

a woman's shoe
bottle of herbal liqueur

benedictine
and the box for

an american-made
sextant

if my plane crashed near nikumaroro
gardner island, in 1937, i would swim
like mad toward land, away from the pull

of metal being sucked into sea. i would swim
and swim and would be too tired to stand
at first, would stare at that spot in the sky

where a plane used to be. a spot he used to
i would suddenly be more thirsty than ever
more than the time i fevered for two months

in toronto. would scoop seawater into cupped
hands to bring to lips. would realize too late
and let it drop through fingers and soak in

would fall soaked into a dream, that i am
a woman in 2020 with a tracking device
that could find me anywhere

they say in hollywood women disappear
after fifty—can only play stock roles
of dutiful wives to well-aging men

cookie-cutter grandmothers. that they
had their picture taken so many times
on the red carpet they form irreversible
sunspots displeasing to the screen

that they stiffen to a still life until
one day you see a memorial picture on
facebook of someone you forgot you knew
doris day dies at 97. and they always show
a picture of the young face there. the part
valued. amelia, you look tired at forty

like you know all about stasis—that this
might be as good as it gets. as you walk
to your plane, your body stiffens to a
stock statue in the middle of the field

Palm tree.

Like crackling icicles,
your brittle sword-branches
rattle in the small breezes
of thick warm nights.

Knowing nothing of cold,
is it with the malice of ignorance,
that you chill
the thick,warm dreams
of souls uneasy at discomfort?

a pilot's a pilot—i hope that such
equality could be carried out in

other fields so that men and women
may achieve equally in any

endeavour they set out
~a.e.

two

in 1799 the first woman soloed. she was jeanne
geneviève garnerin who was the wife of andré-
jacques garnerin, one of the greatest balloonists

of the era. so proficient were the garnerins that
they held the title of official aeronauts to napoleon
when a fluke of fortune deprived them of this position

~(a.e—the fun of it)

each wing actually sends air down by
making a spinning vortex (a kind of mini

tornado) immediately behind it. it's a bit
like when you're standing on a platform

at a railroad station and a high-speed train
rushes past without stopping, leaving what

feels like a huge sucking vacuum in its wake
                                        —how planes work

some of the early paparazzi
capture a photo of you and noonan
on a dock on jaluit island
you are surrounded by locals
and watch as the japanese boat
koshu loads your *electra* as cargo

marshall islanders' legend goes
that fishermen saw the plane go down
and two caucasian fliers emerge
like a birth. a local doctor fixed
wounds on noonan—a head gash
and damaged knees. then as quick
as a developing photo, japanese
swept the plane and the two away
islanders even stamped images of this
as their official postage thirty years ago

that one naval photo, too, goes missing
from the national archive for eighty years

had this happened now
you would have been caught
from every angle, from every pose
as you casually walk in then out
of a local convenience store

i read that before you started to fly, you cut
your long hair and slept in your new leather

jacket for three days, so they would take you
seriously. but even then, you were marketed

sold women's clothing, lucky strikes, luggage
wore *queen of the air,* like a forever sash

did an exhausting circuit, like an 18-hour flight
but even then you were criticized for being too

ambitious, for being underprepared, for taking
too much out of *electra* to fit more fuel, for

not knowing morse code. did you ever feel
that they wanted you to fail. *tom d. crouch*

*senior curator of the national air and space
museum has said that the earhart/noonan*

*electra is '18,000 ft. down and may even
yield a range of artifacts that could rival*

*the find of the titanic,' adding 'the mystery
is part of what keeps us interested. in part*

*we remember her because she's our favourite
missing person'*

12

unsolved mysteries eyewitness account
saipanese woman: nieves cabrera blas

this woman was brought ashore by the
japanese. it was said they had captured
two spy people. the japanese soldiers
brought the spies into town. many of us
went there to see them. the japanese
guards made them take off all their clothes
everything they had on their bodies. it was
then we could see that one of the spies
was a woman. i had never known before
a woman who wore men's trousers. oh
the things that happened to that woman

the soldiers put her in jail. they removed
her jewellry from her hands then the japanese
came and gave her rice. she threw it out

when they took her out of the prison, they tied
her hands. they blindfolded her. i was working
on the farm. i saw a japanese motorcycle. the
woman was in a little seat on the side
of the motorcycle. i watched and they took her
to this place where a hole had been dug. they
made her kneel in front of the hole

i planted a breadfruit tree near her grave

carrion

merciless Life
laughs in the burning sun
and only death,
slow-circling down,
shadows the aerid flesh
bruised by the panther-paws of love.
                    ~emil harte

*after midnight, the moon set, and i
was alone with the stars. i have often
said that the lure of flying is the lure
of beauty, and i need no other flight to
convince me that the reason flyers fly
whether they know it or not, is the
esthetic appeal of flying*

~a.e.

three

*a beautiful and brilliant woman, madame
blanchard was the next incumbent. she was
inducted into office with great ceremony in*

*1810 as napoleon's chief of air service. she
was the widow of the balloonist jean-pierre
blanchard who had been killed in an accident*

*three years before. after his death, she carried
on until she herself became as well known
in france and neighbouring countries as he had*

~(a.e—*the fun of it*)

15

you come to me at 5 a.m., fragments
of stress signals and voice, because you
know it's the best time to get through

so much silence. so much white space
even your bones aren't allowed to speak
for themselves. i prefer to picture you

with the peaceful sway of 18,000 feet
under the pacific instead, because even
then the violence of water invading lungs

seems more natural, because even then
the muted popping sound of parrot fish
feeding on your bones is your own morse

code of the rest of your story untold
i hear you amelia, i really do and in my mind
i plant breadfruit trees near all your graves

every time i fly solo
i end up next to a drunk man
different versions of my father

the young man who drinks and
drinks then tells uncomfortable
jokes until he passes out

the middle-aged man who takes
deep breaths in through his nose
holds that stale air, occasionally
punches it out into the seat
in front of him

the old man with hearing aids
in both ears, who is both gentle
and kind, but who does not open
his eyes until asked if he would
like something to drink

a.e., we have this in common too
do you feel the same, that all you
really want is to relax into flight
without so much emergency fuel

these men, these experts in their field, keep
trying to rescue you, even some 80 years later

the crash and sink theory—99% sure
computers can locate the exact coordinates

of your sunken plane. the gardner island
hypothesis—99% sure the lost bones

are yours, based on an anthropological
database. the japanese capture theory—

99% sure the photo is authentic and that
added with so many eyewitness reports

maybe they carry the dna guilt of *itasca*
radioman leo bellarts, who after said he

was sitting there sweating blood because
i couldn't do a darn thing about it

even when you whistled into the radio
as a surefire way for him to find you

saturday, february 7, 1931

the bride wore brown, and the
groom slipped onto her finger
a plain gold band, which she
never wore afterward
—susan ware

before we are married

you must know   my reluctance   that i shatter
just now   foolish
heart

i shall not hold you   bound

may   keep someplace   to myself

cannot guarantee   the confinement of even
an attractive cage

i must

i will   give you the part of me   you seem to want

a.e.

the poem is written on the letterhead of a hotel:

i have seen your eyes at dawn beloved
dark with sleep
and lying on your breast—have watched
the new day creep

into new depths, putting aside old shadows
spun by night
to show again the lovely living colours
of your sunlit sight

~emil harte

*my ambition is to have this wonderful
gift produce practical results for the future*

*of commercial flying and for the women
who may want to fly tomorrow's planes*

~a.e.

four

*truly she must have been an unusual person for
she combined rugged character and physique
with the charming and delicate exterior demanded*

*of femininity in that period. in the descriptions of
her numerous flights, one is impressed with her
showmanship, her good sense, and her originality*

*she had pluck, too, for she often stayed aloft all
night in her fragile craft and made descents when
morning gave her light*

~(a.e—the fun of it)

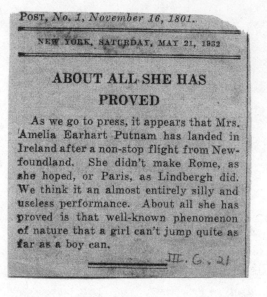

POST, *No. 1, November 16, 1801.*

NEW YORK, SATURDAY, MAY 21, 1932

ABOUT ALL SHE HAS
PROVED

As we go to press, it appears that Mrs. Amelia Earhart Putnam has landed in Ireland after a non-stop flight from New-foundland. She didn't make Rome, as she hoped, or Paris, as Lindbergh did. We think it an almost entirely silly and useless performance. About all she has proved is that well-known phenomenon of nature that a girl can't jump quite as far as a boy can.

III. G. 21

it's a classic story of being
in the wrong place at the wrong

time. you flew right into
the exposition of wwII

became the inciting incident by
being assumed spies, became

prisoners of war. plane burned
bones exhumed, became the

first unofficial american casualties
of war. we still live in a time of

division and power, where it is
easier to cover up the execution-

style truth of things. i'm sorry
you didn't get a happy ending

that you had so many deaths, that
this open denouement forces us

to forever fill in our own version
of an ending only you can tell, but

dirt/water/air forever fills your mouth

a pilot's a pilot—i hope that such
equality could be carried out in other
fields so that men and women may achieve
equally in any endeavour they set out

the imposter syndrome (also known as
imposter phenomenon fraud syndrome or
the imposter experience) marked by an
inability to internalize accomplishments
a pilot's a pilot—i hope that such

they couldn't stop you from getting your
license, from taking lessons or from buying
a plane, but women won't see their first
female pilot at a major u.s. airline until 1973
equality could be carried out in other

but, there's no money in the air shows, so
you have to fly that plane higher, further
just to get noticed. even then, they sit you
in the back of cars and parade you through
fields so that men and women may achieve

a writer's a writer—i hope that such
things will change in my lifetime, that
we can grow out of this narrative of show
me your sex and i'll endorse the illusion—
equally in any endeavor they set out

there are these pivotal moments that
change our trajectory—the fly-float-

fall of when we can see so acute
faster than the speed of sound—

was 1904 that moment for you
when you built a roller-coaster style

ramp from the roof of the toolshed
made a wooden box cart with uncle

that flew off rather than slid down
you emerged from expectation

broken wood. a bruised lip. torn
dress. *oh, pidge, it's just like flying*

From an Airplane.

Even the watchful, purple hills
that hold the lake,
could not see so well as I
the stain of evening
creeping from its heart;
nor the round, yellow eyes of the hamlet
growing filmy with mists.

five

an ascent was a daring commercial spectacle or
a social event. madame blanchard appeared at
affairs where she was bidden by royal command

on this occasion, madame blanchard planned one
of the most spectacular ascents of her career
except in the very earliest experiments hydrogen

had been used to inflate the envelopes of all-sized
balloons. despite knowledge that this gas was
extremely flammable, it had been the custom

more and more frequently to make night ascents
with a display of fireworks lighted on the ground
just before take-off

~(a.e—the fun of it)

if air gives an upward force to a plane,
the plane must give an (equal and opposite)

downward force to the air. so a plane also
generates lift by using its wings to push air

downward behind it. that happens because
the wings aren't perfectly horizontal, as you

might suppose, but tilted back very slightly
so they hit the air at an angle of attack
　　　　　　　　　　　　—how planes work

winged gospel—in this world view
aviation would reorder human society and

promote world peace by breaking down
isolation and distrust. when everyone

took to the air, society would be
transformed along the lines of democracy

freedom, and equality—and perhaps even
women's liberation—Susan Ware

#metoo amelia. i too am *air-minded*
in that every time i see a voice soar

shared and liked, shared and loved
1,260,010 views, i think this is it, #enough

isenough, #timesup, it's happening
but in the same feed, *body of 23-*

year-old missing indigenous woman
pulled from red river

wings make lift by changing the direction
and pressure of air that crashes into them
as the engines shoot them through the sky
                    —how planes work

you underestimate the value of the plane
of how much weight it carries and how
light, how graceful it both flies and falls

you underestimate its design and function
when you catch sight of it—a faraway petite
titanium bird, alive with so many heartbeats

lady lindy—empty wombed
let out some fuel to stay
lean and light in order to fly

lucky lindy—a twenty-month
version of you dismantled
in a field by your home
you sit heavy in the belly
shadow of a boat, then cast
sperm in european fields
to regrow parts of you lost

lady lindy—you are the shadow
of him, cast black and white
on the belly of a transatlantic plane
but as light slowly shifts
it becomes more about you—
flowers held close to womb
you smile for your shot

lucky lindy—epitaph:
if i take the wings of the morning, and
dwell in the uttermost parts of the sea

My Friend.

He has seen clearly;
therefore
irony is his displeasure,
his humor,
and his tenderness.

in those fast-moving days, which have
intervened, the whole width of the world
has passed behind us, except this
broad ocean. i shall be glad when we have
the hazards of its navigation behind us
~a.e.

six

madame blanchard had an extra large framework
hung on the outside of her basket to hold her
assortment. inside her basket she had a special

lighted taper and bomb which she was to set off
when she reached a predetermined altitude. app-
arently there was a leak in the gas-bag over her

head, for when she picked up the taper a flame
shot from it and up the side of the balloon. a
moment afterward her craft began to descend

blazing to earth. chronicles of the day agree she
landed on a house, but differ as to whether she died
from burns or because of a fall from the roof

~(a.e—the fun of it)

did they feed you breadfruit—
grapefruit-sized breasts

plucked from a tree that has
both male and female parts

the ripe fruit soaked then baked
like bread. slipped through bars

of a cell no bigger than a cockpit
your stomach churns, it churns

the texture of it rises
full pockets of air

it feeds you, but it doesn't
they feed you, but they don't

even though you were never there
when your body lay dormant

they stripped it for parts, for
keeps. peeled off words

until there were none
not one scrap left

not one bone—you
were never there

we are still trying to get ourselves
called just 'pilots'

sweetheart of the air
girl flyer

bird woman
girl thrilled by adventure

lady lindy
girl's plane fueled for atlantic start

feminine ace
girl on atlantic hop

heroine of the skies
girl lindy's triumph

first lady of the air
girl flyer in london

premier aviatrix
epochal moments in career of girl flyer

no. 1 ladybird
powder-puff derby

helen richey   painfully   in 1934

beat out seven male competitors for a position
          as co-pilot on central airways

                    pilots were unhappy about a female
                              invading the male bastion

     of the cockpit   implying richey was too weak

this is pilot richey. yes, she's a girl. she's young. she's pretty

                              the aeronautics bureau issued

an advisory, limiting women to fair-weather flying

grounding female pilots for nine days during menstruation

                    she resigned   in 1935

To M ——— .

Like your body's beauty
the humor of your frankness
pleased them-- who saw the surface only,
nor saw you
laughing at them with a wistful scorn
and eyes of cool intelligence.

[women] must pay for everything

they do get more glory than men
for comparable feats. but, also, women
get more notoriety when they crash
~a.e.

seven

the next important name in the nineteenth century
gives us among women balloonists is not a new one
the family of garnerin again comes to the fore in

the person of elisa, a niece of the original andre-
jacques. she stands out from the other aeronauts
of the day because she undertook to make parachute

descents. she went aloft sitting in a little basket
attached to a parachute which in turn hung from
one balloon. when the moment came to cut off

she released a rope and settled earthward, where she
willed. possessed of a good deal of energy, she toured
europe extensively, giving her special exhibitions

~*(a.e—the fun of it)*

39

in may 1927—when you sit in the
gender neutral dark of a theatre and
the newsreel picture stutters on to

reveal the his and hers of the crowd
a man that looks eerily like you steps
into his flight suit, steps into his *spirit*

of st. louis, you uncross your legs
lean in to the black and white thrust
of air as the plane wobbles, the roll

the hop and then the lift, your
shoulders lean forward on take off
elbows on knees in a group of people

who don't yet know who you are, you
could blend in, could be taken for a
his—you could make this flight too

here i am jumping through
hoops just like the little white
horse in the circus—a.e.

fuck me, i am trying so hard

to be whole for you, and for you, and for you
and don't worry, i didn't forget about you

it's just that i know *you* can hold
the weight of your own head right now

so i'll come back—i promise—
please don't slap me with that sigh

that overt silence—soaked water heavy with
i am not enough. i've heard it before

i wrote that poem. am writing it still
can you please come back later today

perhaps you will see me do this trick where
i hold the shadow of a woman on my toes

if you've ever stood near a helicopter, you'll know
exactly how it stays in the sky: it creates a huge
"downwash" (downward moving draft) of air that

balances its weight. helicopter rotors are very similar
to airplane airfoils, but spin around in a circle instead
of moving forward in a straight line, like the ones on a

plane. even so, airplanes create downwash in exactly
the same way as helicopters—it's just that we don't notice
the downwash isn't so obvious, but it's just as important
                                   —how planes work

this photograph of amelia earhart in an
open cockpit was taken two years before
the 1928 flight. the juxtaposition of the

cap and goggles with the pearls certainly
catches the viewer's attention, as do the
beauty and strength of the aviator's gaze
                                    —susan ware

amelia, you understand 'downwash'
balancing the weight of *his* and *hers*
—of beauty and strength—you have

no problem starring down the lens
full force—unapologetic of your sex
even though you privately write

poetry, you pen it with the *his* alias
emil harte. even though you honor
the pilot's uniform—jodhpurs, riding

boots, leather jacket, you add silk
even after nineteen hours in the air
her silk scarf is perfectly knotted

and she seemed totally in control
you know how these things work

courage is the price that life exacts for granting peace.
the soul that knows it not, knows no release
from little things;

knows not the livid loneliness of fear
nor mountain heights, where bitter joy can hear
the sound of wings.

how can life grant us boon of living, compensate
for dull grey ugliness and pregnant hate
unless we dare

the soul's dominion? each time we make a choice, we pay
with courage to behold resistless day
and count it fair.

the stars seemed near enough to
touch and never before have i seen

so many. i always believed the lure
of flying is the lure of beauty, but i

was sure of it that night
~a.e.

eight

england produced the next well-known woman
balloonist. her name was margaret graham, and
she was different from madame blanchard or mlle

garnerin as anyone possibly could be. in the first
place, she combined domesticity and a career in
a more than modern manner. she was the mother

of seven children and she managed to make
exhibitions over all england and keep her home
in london going at the same time

~(a.e—the fun of it)

when locals looked toward the sea

that day, they thought it was a wall
of rain coming in with the wind, with

the surf, but really it was five thousand
signed stamp covers—presold by putnam

for five dollars each—they littered
the crux of trees, boats on the beach

with inches of water still at the feet
but only served well to start the fires

to start the boil, to soften the bread-
fruit, to feed the children, who made

rudimentary planes with some that
fell, soft like feathers, slightly folded

in order to really, truly fly

your skin would need to be stretched
so thin, to reach the torque, the tip

the balance. bones shaped by wind
but, *oh, pidge,* that body would climb

zoom, 45 bank, stall, vertical bank
glide, dive 38 spiral, tailspin, side

slip, split 's' turn, forward slip
barrel roll, loop inside, loop outside

until all that is left is debris on a beach
—they wonder, wonder if it is yours

did you ever feel you were flying

too high and that the whole thing
could blow apart. bolts fall like

ice chips. aluminum peels back
dials spin and spin until they hit

ground. you left holding a control
wheel. a seat left holding air

'ninety-nines have a friend in every airport'—

we women pilots have a rough, rocky road
ahead of us. men do not believe us capable

we can fly—you know that. ever since we started
we've butted our heads against a stone wall

manufacturers refuse us planes, the public
have no confidence in our ability. if we had

access to the equipment and training men have
we could certainly do as well. thank heaven, we

continue willingly fighting a losing battle…but if
enough of us keep trying, we'll get someplace

~a.e.

> *i have a feeling that there is just*
> *about one more good flight left in*
> *my system, and i hope this trip is it*
> ~a.e.

nine

mrs graham had her share of mishaps. once
she landed in the sea of plymoth when a strong
wind bore her away from shore. another time

she had the misfortune to displace with her
dangling grappling hook a piece of stone coping
which fell to the street and killed a pedestrian

~(a.e—*the fun of it*)

we tried in vain to have him alter the
course of the roosevelt and land in some
pleasant country where no one knew us

for all three of us dreaded the inevitable
receptions and longed for the ocean to
stretch itself indefinitely
                              ~a.e.

they say that most people die
in a tsunami because they are stuck

mesmerized by the size of the wave
or when being charged by a crimson bear

stunned by the twitch of each red muscle engaged
or the warm movement of an entire mountain on fire

was it like that for you—nose pointed to waves
were you able to pick out patterns of light

that stretched then stretched then stretched
as far as you could see. did you smile

you feel as though you're falling, feel the
push of air parachute your wide-legged pants

feel the pull toward the rooftops of tiny houses
below and know that sick feeling in your stomach

that this is what was expected of you all along
you make the shape of an X with your body

count the seconds of shallow breath in and then
out, in and watch bits of you rip off and fly up

watch a molted crow glide smooth, parallel
lean in and pluck a hair from your head, think

oh pidge, it's just like flying, lean in towards
a body of water, pull yourself together to brace

for it. your feet break the skin and then you sink
and sink and sink with the bodies of other women

a sextant, a woman's shoe and a bottle of herbal
liqueur. lined at the bottom of a sand-soft end

are the most beautiful hot air balloons stretched
open, waiting, waiting, willing you to land

in 1977, seven days after i was born, when
my mother still attempted a firm latch
on breasts that would never produce
enough milk, as i got smaller and small-
er and small, president gerald ford
pardoned iva toguri of treason—

renounced the label of *tokyo rose*
and allowed her to regain american
citizenship that had been stripped for thirty-
five years, but not before *orphan ann* was
detained for a year by the u.s. then
held in prison for six out of ten years
for soaring her american accent
over southern pacific airways

did you know: toguri graduated from
u.c.l.a in 1940. when an aunt fell ill
she went to japan, leaving l.a.
with only an i.d. card

she tried to get a passport in japan
but was unable to before pearl harbour

labelled an enemy of japan, toguri was denied
a food ration card. her family banished her

she became a broadcaster on a japanese show
called "the zero hour". did you know
that she used the money to smuggle food
to prisoners of war. did you know that

on september 29, 1949 the jury found toguri
guilty on a single charge: *'on a day during october
1944, the exact date being to the grand jurors
unknown, said defendant at tokyo japan, in a
studio of the broadcasting corporation, did
speak into a microphone concerning the loss of ships'*

did you know this is about hunger

did you know the witnesses lied

amelia, amelia to tokyo rose
amelia, amelia to tokyo rose

do you copy, do you copy

noses pressed to concrete
they speak to one another

like trying to push sound
through water. the english

as comforting as hot food
are you there. are you still

there. i hear you. i hear you

ironically, the strategy of using women
to break down the fear of flying paved
the way for the rise of the stewardess,
the one job in aviation where women
were truly welcome—susan ware

one job went   to women:

                                        had to be

unmarried, small (no more than 120 pounds and five
feet four)

under the age of twenty-five

                              their main function to
            pamper   male passengers

                              the all–american girl
                    would help calm the air

        just another nurturing function to domesticate

women are seeking freedom. freedom

in the skies!...the woman at the washtub
the sewing machine, the office desk, and

the typewriter can glance up from the
window when she hears the rhythmic hum

of a motor overhead, and say, 'if it's a
woman she is helping free me, too!'

—margery brown (1930)
journalist & amateur flyer

the most difficult thing is the decision
to act. the rest is merely tenacity. the fears
are paper tigers. you can do anything
you decide to do.
~a.e.

ten

i have said little concerning the clothes of 'the only
female aeronaut' of victoria's reign, as mrs.
graham called herself. it is easy to see
that ballooning offered to her and her sisters

limitless scope for the use of all kinds of furbelows
not only was the person of the aeronaut decorated
but the craft as well. the beplumed and beribboned
equipages were designed to harmonize with and

enhance the appearances of the performers. and
vice versa. the silks and satins of the day carried
right over into the very business of ballooning. it
seems almost as if the spectacular side of aerial

entertainment has never reached so high a pinnacle as
it did during this fabulous period of balloon pageantry

~(a.e—the fun of it)

the four forces are unbalanced
during take-off, climbing, descending
maneuvering, landing, or basically anytime
the airplane is not cruising. an object at rest
will stay at rest. an object in motion will stay
in motion at a constant velocity until acted
upon by an outside force
—nasa: beginners guide to aerodynamics
cruising aircraft and balanced forces

flying is so much about balance, and
that's it, really. that feeling that at
any moment i could fall out of this sky
woman/mother/writer/teacher, particles of
debris and it forces acids from my stomach up
the slosh of an almost empty tank, forces
a kind of slight correction, to account for
the pressure both pushing/pulling—this
lift, thrust, drag and weight

really, you escaped and hitched a boat ride
back to the states. lived renamed, like iva did,
in new jersey, until you were 90, didn't you

your grandchildren rested their well fed
bellies on the bottoms of your feet as you
pushed your legs in the air, held their arms

out and let them fly. they thought you were
shy with cameras because you were a woman
who came from nothing—from a time and place

when women didn't look up—who spun
stories from the books you read with pidge—
in yours pidge is jean and she died when she

was a nurse in the war. you lived in peace
avoided newspaper theories in checkout stands
kneaded sourdough bread, whistled like wind

watched it rise. flew in your dreams—arms out-
stretched. wrote so many poems from that place
oh man, irene's quite the imagination. she writes

the real mccoy, as though she was there. no joke

i have an image—while you fly low
after the radio cuts out, after the engines

cut out, in those seconds of glide
a trade wind turns you around and

you are carried on the backs of
hundreds of crows back to papua

new guinea. there, the locals circle
you like a womb, they circle your

neck with flowers. *electra* rests in the
jungle, overgrows with a green vine

that the children can climb. in
circle stories, at night, around fire

you tell the young girls about places
you have been, spin beautiful poetic

phrases into the sky. you tell them
about records you broke, about books

you wrote, about birth control and
the vote. you teach them how to fly

birds carry story fragments and ash
circumnavigate the globe and drop

their feathers in backyards around
the world, where for the past eighty

years children climb into makeshift
planes and pretend they are you

"faint signals heard from amelia's plane"

cloudy weather, cloudy

we must be on you, but
we cannot see you. fuel
is running low. been
unable to reach you by
radio. we are flying at
1,000 feet

we are running
north and south

epilogue

how to survive if your parachute fails to open

step 1: don't panic   keep your wits
                                    concentrate

regulate   breathing   clear your mind   inhale deeply

                step 2: spread your body in an X
                get as flat as possible

                        achieve the most drag you can
                        arch your head and back

step 3: aim for marshy, wooded or snowy areas

      avoid hard objects like concrete, buildings or flat fields

                  steer left or right by lowering your elbow
            lean   in the direction   you want

step 4: get in the skydiver's landing stance
        land on your feet
            flex both your knees and hips

                step 5: if you must land in water
           tighten your body and fall feet first
     hands to your sides

                step 6: land on your feet
                        you may injure your legs or hips

                                step 7: protect your head
                                and roll if you can
                                doing a somersault may help

Source Materials

—the following references are accessible by way of QR codes or the tinyurl.com links.

pp. 1-2 – "Prologue" erasure poem from the video "How to Survive An Airplane Crash" tinyurl.com/Lady-Bird-p2

p. 3 – *"one"* found poem from the chapter "The First Women Aeronauts" in *The Fun of It*, written by Amelia Earhart, p. 194

p. 5 – found poem from news article "Bones found on Pacific island belong to Amelia Earhart, scientist claims" in CTV news, written by Josh K. Elliott, March 8, 2018 tinyurl.com/Lady-Bird-P5

p. 8 – "palm tree" poem written by Amelia Earhart, found at Purdue University E-Archives tinyurl.com/Lady-Bird-P8

p. 9 – *"two"* found poem from the chapter "The First Women Aeronauts" in *The Fun of It*, written by Amelia Earhart, p. 194

p. 10 – found poem from the website: "How Planes Work" tinyurl.com/Lady-Bird-P10

p. 12 – quote from "Amelia Earhart" in "Wikipedia"
tinyurl.com/Lady-Bird-P12

p. 13 – "unsolved mysteries eyewitness account of
saipanese woman: nieves cabrera blas" is a found
poem from "Unsolved Mysteries with Robert Stack
- Season 3, Episode 8" found on YouTube
tinyurl.com/Lady-Bird-P13

p. 14 – "carrion" poem by Amelia Earhart, found in
the article "What Archives Reveal: The Hidden Poems
of Amelia Earhart" written by Sammie L. Morris
tinyurl.com/Lady-Bird-P14a

p. 15 – "*three*" found poem from the chapter "The First Women
Aeronauts" in *The Fun of It*, written by Amelia Earhart, p. 195

p. 18 – quote from "Amelia Earhart" in "Wikipedia"
tinyurl.com/Lady-Bird-P18

p.19 – erasure poem from a letter written to George Putnam,
by Amelia Earhart, as a form of a prenuptial agreement, found
in "A Modern Woman Makes History" in *Still Missing: Amelia
Earhart and the Search for Modern Feminism*, written by Susan
Ware, p. 50-51

p. 20 – "the poem is written on the letterhead of a hotel:"
poem by Amelia Earhart, found in the article "What Archives

Reveal: The Hidden Poems of Amelia Earhart"
written by Sammie L. Morris
tinyurl.com/Lady-Bird-P20

p. 21 – "*four*" found poem from the chapter "The First Women
Aeronauts" in *The Fun of It*, written by Amelia Earhart, p. 196

p. 22 – "About All She Has Proved" a news article
from May 21, 1932 about Amelia Earhart, found at
Purdue University E-Archives
tinyurl.com/Lady-Bird-P22

p. 25 – "*oh, pidge, it's just like flying*" quote from
"Amelia Earhart" in "Wikipedia"
tinyurl.com/Lady-Bird-P25

p. 26 – "From an Airplane" poem written by Amelia
Earhart, found at Purdue University E-Archives
tinyurl.com/QR-LadyBird-P26

p. 27 – "*five*" found poem from the chapter "The First Women
Aeronauts" in *The Fun of It*, written by Amelia Earhart, p. 196

p. 28 – found poem quoted from: "How Planes
Work"
tinyurl.com/Lady-Bird-P28

p. 29 – quote from "A Modern Woman Makes History" in *Still Missing: Amelia Earhart and the Search for Modern Feminism*, written by Susan Ware, p. 62, and headline from "Body of missing woman April Carpenter pulled from Red River" CBC news article from May 17, 2018 tinyurl.com/Lady-Bird-P29

p. 30 – quote from: "How Planes Work" tinyurl.com/Lady-Bird-P30

p. 31 – "*if i take the wings of the morning, and dwell in the uttermost parts of the sea*" Epitaph for Charles Lindbergh. It is from Psalms 139:9

p. 32 – "My Friend" poem written by Amelia Earhart, found at Purdue University E-Archives tinyurl.com/Lady-Bird-P32

p. 33 – "*six*" found poem from the chapter "The First Women Aeronauts" in *The Fun of It*, written by Amelia Earhart, p. 197

p. 36 – newsreel titles, found in "Iconography and Representation" in *Still Missing: Amelia Earhart and the Search for Modern Feminism*, written by Susan Ware, p. 152

p. 37 – erasure poem from "Gender and Aviation" in *Still Missing: Amelia Earhart and the Search for Modern Feminism*, written by Susan Ware, p. 76-77

p. 38 – "To M——" poem written by Amelia Earhart, found at Purdue University E-Archives
tinyurl.com/QR-LadyBird-P38

p. 39 – "*seven*" found poem from the chapter "The First Women Aeronauts" in *The Fun of It*, written by Amelia Earhart, p. 197

p. 42 – found poem quoted from: "How Planes Work"
tinyurl.com/Lady-Bird-P42

p. 43 – quoted from "Iconography and Representation" in *Still Missing: Amelia Earhart and the Search for Modern Feminism*, written by Susan Ware, p. 154

p. 44 – "Courage" poem by Amelia Earhart, found in *Last Flight: Amelia Earhart's Flying Adventures* written by Amelia Earhart, p. 227

p. 45 – "*eight*" found poem from the chapter "The First Women Aeronauts" in *The Fun of It*, written by Amelia Earhart, p. 198

p. 46 – "Amelia Earhart on Aircraft and Needle-craft" found at Purdue University E-Archives
tinyurl.com/Lady-Bird-P46

p. 50 – quoted from Earhart in "Gender and Aviation" in *Still Missing: Amelia Earhart and the Search for Modern Feminism*, written by Susan Ware, p. 89

p. 51 – "*nine*" found poem from the chapter "The First Women Aeronauts" in *The Fun of It*, written by Amelia Earhart, p. 199

p. 52 – quoted from "Across the Atlantic with the Friendship," in *The Fun of It*, written by Amelia Earhart, p. 86

p. 55 – quoted from "Iva Toguri D'Aquino and 'Tokyo Rose'"
tinyurl.com/Lady-Bird-P55

p. 57 – erasure poem from "Gender and Aviation" in *Still Missing: Amelia Earhart and the Search for Modern Feminism*, written by Susan Ware, p. 74 & 87

p. 58 – quoted by Margery Brown in "Gender and Aviation" in *Still Missing: Amelia Earhart and the Search for Modern Feminism*, written by Susan Ware, p. 63

p. 59 – "*ten*" found poem from the chapter "The First Women Aeronauts" in *The Fun of It*, written by Amelia Earhart, p. 201

p. 60 – quoted from "Nasa: A Beginners Guide to Aerodynamics"
tinyurl.com/Lady-Bird-P60

p. 64 – found poem from "Amelia Earhart Disappears Near Howland Island" in "World History Project"
tinyurl.com/Lady-Bird-P64

pp. 65-66 – "epilogue" erasure poem from "How to Survive if Your Parachute Fails to Open" in "Wiki How"
tinyurl.com/Lady-Bird-P65

ACKNOWLEDGEMENTS

Thank you: Amelia, for coming to me at 5 a.m. to help write these poems.

Thank you: Okanagan College, for the funding and time to make the collection possible.

Thank you: Michael Callaghan, publisher and books designer at Exile Editions, for the precision and artistry you brought to this process. Marsha Boulton, I appreciate your keen editing acumen.

Thank you: writing friends and mentors, for continued inspiration and support: kevin mchpherson eckhoff, Mona Fertig, Penn Kemp, John Lent, Melissa Munn, Al Rempel, Sharon Thesen, Clare Thiessen.

Thank you: Poetry in Canada crew, for dreaming big with me – some of the kindest, most thoughtful people I know: JP Baker, Otoniya Okot Bitek, Rina Chua, Stephen Collis, James Gifford, Theresa Rogers, Renée Sarojini Saklikar.

Thank you: Spokes, for being everything – talented, beautiful humans: Natalie Appleton, Hannah Calder, Michelle Doege, Kristin Froneman, Karen Meyer, Laisha Rosnau.

Thank you: family who is family and friends who are family, for supporting me in this wonderful poetic life. I am lucky to know you.

Thank you: reader, for your generosity.

Kerry Gilbert lives in the Okanagan, where she teaches Creative Writing at Okanagan College. Her first book, *(kerplnk): a verse novel of development*, was published in 2005. Her second book of poetry, *Tight Wire*, was published in 2016. *Little Red* is Gilbert's most recent poetry collection, released in 2019. Gilbert has won the Gwendolyn MacEwen Poetry Award for Best Suite by an Emerging Writer, has been shortlisted for ReLit, for the Ralph Gustafson Prize for the Best Poem, the Pacific Spirit Poetry Contest, and the Gwendolyn MacEwen Poetry for Best Suite by an Established Writer. www.kerrygilbert.ca

Photograph by Silmara Emde